The Ghostly Tales of Nashua, New Hampshire

Published by Arcadia Children's Books
A Division of Arcadia Publishing, Inc.
Charleston, SC
www.arcadiapublishing.com

First published 2025
Manufactured in the United States

Designed by Jessica Nevins
Images used courtesy of Shutterstock.com and Susanna Hargreaves.

ISBN: 9781467195997
Library of Congress Control Number: 2025932963

Spooky America

The Ghostly Tales of Nashua, New Hampshire

Susanna Hargreaves

arcadia
CHILDREN'S BOOKS

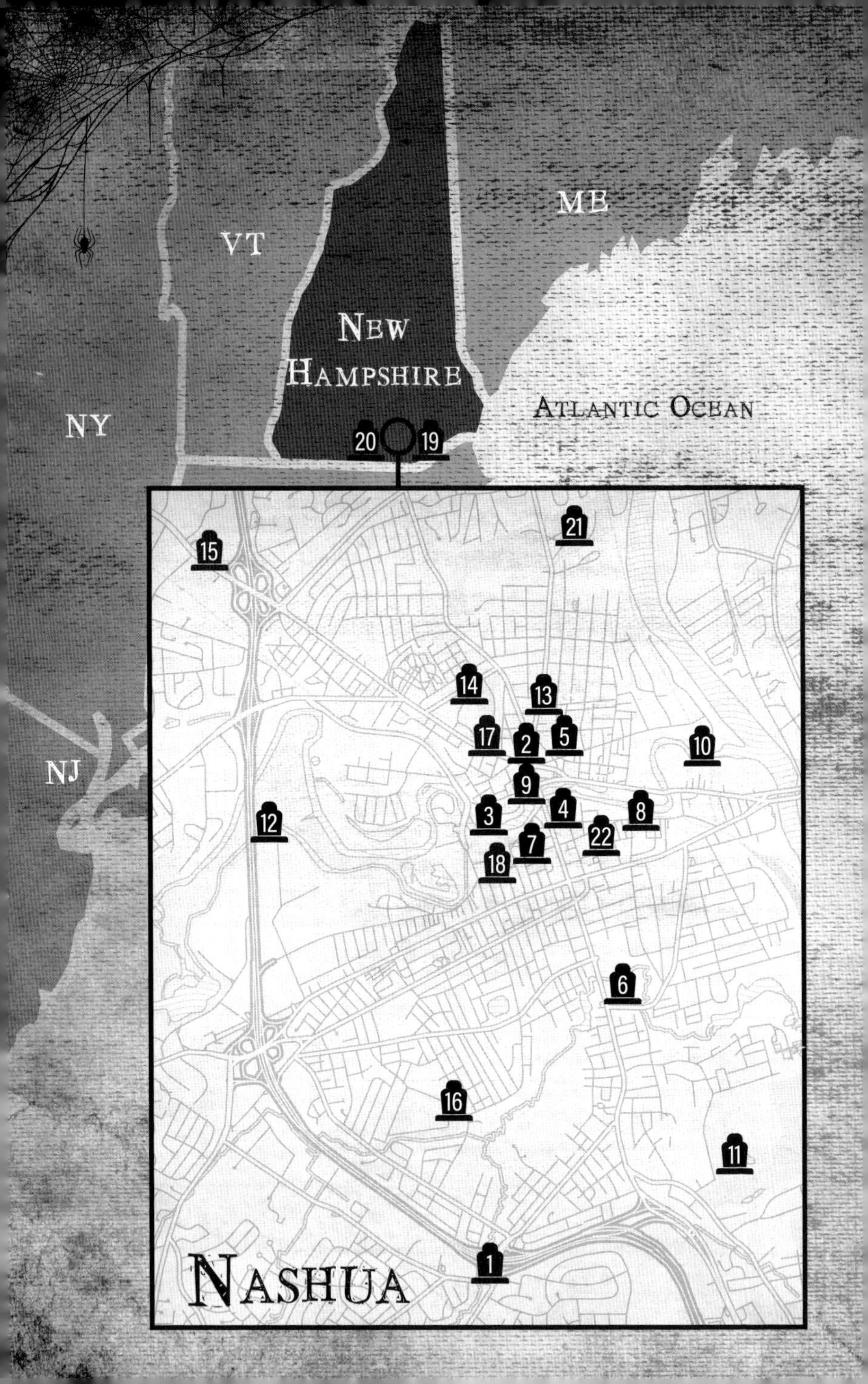
VT
ME
NY
NJ
New Hampshire
Atlantic Ocean
Nashua
20
19
21
15
14
13
17
2
5
10
9
3
4
8
12
7
22
18
6
16
11
1

Table of Contents & Map Key

Nashua, New Hampshire

Foreword

Growing up in Nashua was like being in a big playground that just happened to have a haunted house—or a bunch of them, really. Picture this: bikes flying down the streets, loud laughs echoing like we were in a sitcom, playing ball with the crew, and thinking we were gonna be the next big football stars. And don't even get me started on those hot summer nights at Hayward's, where ice cream was the fix for everything! Between the ice cream cones, arcade games at Fun World, or an epic game of hoops, there was another side of Nashua to explore.

This book? Well, it's a road trip back to those days. It's a wild ride through the haunts of Nashua, where our history meets the spooky.

Enjoy the read!

—Mike Koutrobis

Comedian and Proud Nashua Native

Gilson Road Cemetery

Welcome to Spooky Nashua, New Hampshire!

The city of Nashua, New Hampshire, is full of fascinating history, and it also has some ghostly surprises! If you are feeling brave, come along with me as we explore some ghostly tales hidden in the shadows of this lively New England city. These stories are meant just for fun, but I must warn you; they are inspired by real events and people! Each story comes from old tales, old newspapers, personal interviews, and treasures found in libraries and the Nashua Historical Society.

First, did you know that Nashua used to be a part of Massachusetts? It's true! Long ago, Nashua wasn't even called Nashua. It was known as Dunstable, a frontier town first settled in the 1640s. However, this land was already home to the Pennacook people, part of the larger Abenaki tribe, who lived throughout the region. Led by the respected Chief Passaconaway and his son Wannalancit, the Pennacook hunted, fished, and grew crops along the rivers. They shared their knowledge of the land, teaching settlers to plant corn, fish, and hunt deer.

However, life was challenging and conflicts grew. From 1675 to 1725, the area became known as "the front of danger," with the King Philip's War and Queen Anne's War bringing more hardship and fear. The settlers built strong, fortress-like garrison houses close together to help protect each other from danger. Over time, more families moved to the area.

According to historical texts, it took a long time for the residents to agree on a name for the town. After being Dunstable, it became Indian

Head Village, named after a warrior who left a carving on a tree. It then expanded into small villages: Centre Village, where Rivier University now stands; Indian Head Village, known today as Library Hill; and Harbour Village near Salmon Brook.

According to an old book, *The History of Nashua*, in 1801, a turnpike road made it easier to travel to Boston, making it a busy route for stagecoaches and farmers. Then, in 1803, a canal boat named "The Nashua" was launched, marking the start of Nashua's industrial growth with mills and factories along the rivers. Disagreements over the town hall's location even led Nashua to split temporarily, with the area north of the Main Street bridge becoming Nashville, while the south stayed Nashua.

Finally, in 1853, the two sides reunited as the City of Nashua, now known as "Gate City," for its importance in New Hampshire. Today, Nashua's history lives on in its old buildings and maybe even in the ghosts that are still rumored to wander its streets!

So let's explore some of this mysterious history. Together, we will learn there are still locations that hold powerful stories from long ago, like the Hassell Family Monument and the place that was once the Nashua Poor Farm. There is a haunted library, the spooky bridge, a skeleton under an old school, and the tragic tale of the wailing woman on Factory Street. Discover an old cemetery rumored to be haunted by the ghosts of the warriors from the Abenaki tribe and wander through the tombstones of the Old South Burying Ground where the earliest settlers rest. Learn a few Abenaki ghostly legends and folklore that haunt our forests. Some of these places may seem hidden, but they are still here to remind us of the past. Listen closely and pay attention, for their stories matter to this day. And some still have a warning for us from the grave!

Through the years, I have enjoyed learning about the history of Nashua. These ghostly tales are a part of local folklore and provide cultural expression, historical preservation, and social entertainment. As an educator and parent, I believe storytelling is a wonderful art and pastime.

Not only can ghost stories give us an interesting connection to our past, we can learn so much from our local legends and lore.

Whether you are a believer in ghosts or not, I hope these historic tales will entertain and inspire discussion and further exploration. So, if you're seeking thrills or simply looking to learn some spooky history of Nashua, these tales are yours to enjoy and pass on for generations to come.

Nashua is full of so many great stories. Who knows what story may haunt you? Are you ready to hear some spine-tingling tales and spooky history? Let's begin!

Part 1: Ghostly Tales of Old Homes and Businesses

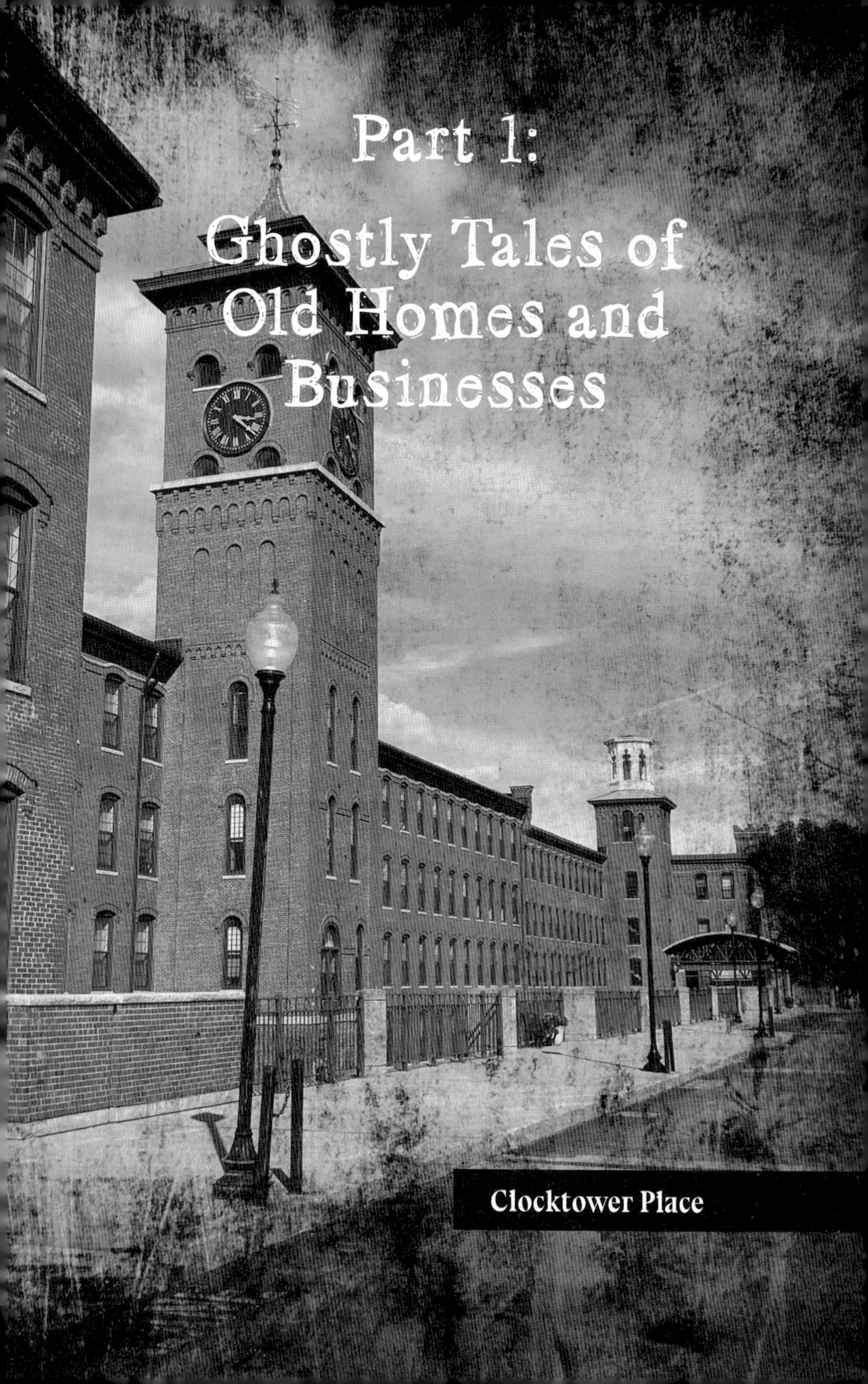

Clocktower Place

"All houses wherein men have lived and died are haunted houses."

—*Haunted Houses* by
Henry Wadsworth Longfellow (1858)

The Thomas Killicut House

CHAPTER 1

The Spirit of the Oldest House in Nashua

In the southern part of the city stands the most historic home in Nashua. Furthermore, it is the last surviving home from the colonial era in the entire city. Known as the Killicut House, this cozy Cape-style home is wrapped in local legend, and for many years, people called it "The 1700 House."

According to the history of the home, the first known owner was Thomas Killicut, a brave man who lived during the town's early days. He moved to what is now Nashua in 1746 and became a field driver, an official who rounds up roaming farm animals for safekeeping. During a time when many farmers let their livestock roam, field drivers took care of lost animals such as horses, goats, sheep, and pigs. Killicut was also part of a group of daring soldiers who fought in the French and Indian War. His son, also named Thomas, would eventually become a soldier in the Revolutionary War.

Over time, much of the land surrounding the house was divided up, and newer homes were built nearby.

Some say the house still holds stories from the past, and if you listen carefully, you might just hear them. The owners know the spirit of the house well, and they believe it is very happy with the renovations and love they have put into the home. When the house was purchased in 1982, it was greatly in need of renovation and repair. During these renovations, the new owners paid a historical architect to visit and analyze the home. They learned from the style of the building and materials in the front room in the original part of the house that it was built around 1680–1700, and the rest of the house was completed before 1730.

The owners confessed that they felt and believed there was a presence in the house when they first moved in. "The house spirit seemed to sigh in relief that someone was there to take care of the home. I think he seemed grateful we were there and wanted us to care for it."

The owners explained how the house is so old that the worn, crooked doors will sometimes open and shut on their own. When a door shuts, they often joke and say, "Hi, Mr. Killicut." Thankfully, he never answers.

During the renovations, the owners discovered many old objects from colonial times. They found an old wooden nail, a wooden cobbler's device, a small pottery pitcher, and a weaving tool. The most interesting object discovered in the wall panel next to the fireplace was an old pair of brown leather children's shoes!

According to superstitions during colonial times, this tradition of protection was to place shoes under the floorboards and in the walls near fireplaces or the door openings to ward off evil spirits and bring good fortune. The owners feel that it worked because their family has been very happy in their "dear old home."

The old children's shoes found in the wall. According to colonial folklore, shoes were placed in the wall for protection and good luck.

CHAPTER 2

The Old Haunted Library

At the top of Main Street in Nashua stands the Hunt Memorial Building, a historic structure built in 1903. Over the years, people have whispered that the building might be haunted. Staff, visitors, and contractors have reported strange experiences such as cold spots, mysterious footsteps, doors creaking open by themselves, the strong feelings of being watched, and more!

According to the history of the building, the Hunt Memorial Building was originally the city library. It was designed by a famous architect named Ralph Adams Cram, and it was built thanks to the kindness of Mary A. and Mary E. Hunt, the wife and daughter of John M. Hunt, a local businessman. The library closed in 1971. Later, it served as offices for the school district before becoming a city space for events.

Amy, the property manager for the past decade, has seen and heard many things she just can't explain.

One day, while taking out the trash, Amy turned around and saw a teenage boy with red hair wearing a yellow plaid shirt standing in the stairway. He smiled at her, then vanished.

But that's not all. Amy has also heard a male voice call her name when no one is around. Doors open on their own, lights turn on by themselves, and a wicker chair has moved in the basement, as if by unseen hands. There's also a small piano music box that mysteriously plays by itself.

According to Amy, most of these strange happenings seem to take place in the fall and winter months and whenever there are contractors doing renovations. Contractors have reported hearing footsteps and voices when no one else is there. One even felt a tug on his shirt while standing on a ladder.

One morning, the activity was so intense that Amy called the police, thinking someone had broken in. The motion-sensor lights in the restroom were on. After checking the building, the police found no one there.

Renters here have also experienced strange things, like hearing footsteps upstairs and finding no one there. One reported seeing the same red-haired boy that Amy described.

One time, ghost hunters visited the building and recorded a voice telling them to "keep it down." They wondered if it was a ghost of the library making sure it was quiet for those who wished to read. Don't forget to return your book!

Despite these eerie events, Amy says the spirits seem friendly. She believes they are just stopping by to check on the place from time to time. She loves the building and isn't frightened by the ghosts. They've become part of the Hunt Memorial's story.

CHAPTER 3

The Ghosts of Clocktower Place

In the heart of Nashua, right by the river, there's a historic building that seems to hold many secrets. It's called Clocktower Place, and from the outside, it might just look like a bunch of old buildings. But long ago, these buildings were home to the Nashua Manufacturing Company, a busy factory where thousands of hardworking citizens earned their living. Now, these beautifully renovated buildings are home to nearly 1,000 people.

Some say the spirits of those who once lived and worked in the building have never really left.

According to the book *The Nashua Experience: History in the Making 1673-1978*, these mill buildings and their workers were an important part of the economic growth in the city. In 1822, a Harvard-educated lawyer and prominent investor named Daniel Abbot noticed that the Nashua River was the perfect place for building textile mills. He asked his friends to join his endeavor, including his law partner Benjamin French, a shopkeeper named Joseph Greeley, and Moses Tyler, who owned a tavern. In 1823, Daniel Abbot and his partners chartered the Nashua Manufacturing Company, which became one of the largest producers of blankets in the world. This mill employed many Irish and French-Canadian immigrants.

According to the Nashua Historical Society, more women—and also children—were hired because they were less costly to employ. Young children had important jobs, like handling the bobbins, which were large spools of thread used to make cloth. The children would carry full bobbins to the weaving room, placing them near the machines that turned thread into fabric. Then, they'd collect the empty bobbins and return them to be rewound. Because children were smaller in size, they could fit underneath the machines to retrieve items that were dropped. Just like the adults, these kids worked all day, too.

How old are you? Can you imagine having to work all day and not be able to go to school?

Working at the mill offered a chance to earn money, but history tells us that it was dangerous.

On July 1, 1856, there was a tragic fire in Mill Building One that broke out in the spinning room from the friction of machinery. According to the book by Judge Edward Parker, *The History of Nashua,* published in 1897, "The fire took at noon, while the help were at dinner, except two women who were driven by the flames to the roof, from which, in their fright they jumped and were killed."

Children were also often injured on the job. On November 9, 1880, *The Nashua Telegraph* reported, "Johnny Chambeau, a small lad, got caught in some mule machinery at the Nashua company's mills this morning by which his head was considerably injured. He will probably be all right again in a few days."

On April 15, 1899, also according to the *Telegraph*, a teenaged French boy named Joseph Peuo was "fearfully, if not fatally," injured one morning in an elevator accident that struck the back of his neck. "It was found he was paralyzed below his neck and he cannot live twenty-four hours. It is a sad accident, as the boy's widowed mother is very poor."

There were other tales of tragedy. On August 21, 1899, another article reported how the malaria epidemic had spread through Nashua, affecting many mill workers. The first death was eighteen-year-old Arinini Cote, and four other members of her family also became sick. Around 150 mill workers were affected by this terrible illness.

There was also a great deal of social unrest due to the harsh working conditions. In 1915, workers at the Nashua Manufacturing Company went on strike, demanding better wages and a longer lunch break. The strike started in October and lasted into the following spring, marked by rising tensions and violence.

The strike began when some workers brought their complaints to the mill bosses. The situation quickly escalated, and on October 5, the mill shut down. The next day, the streets around the mill were filled with strikes. Crowds clashed with the police, who struggled to keep the peace.

Things turned very violent when the militia shot a man named Adam Rasavitch during a confrontation, and several women were injured. As tensions rose in Nashua, there were more incidents of violence, including the death of another worker named Jim Stivie as he left a different mill, the Jackson Company. Stivie was only twenty-five years old and, sadly, left behind a wife and children.

Four years after receiving a government award for service to the military during World War II, the mill closed in 1948. Then another company took over. According to an article in the *Telegraph*, a night watchman was on his way to the mill's roof to watch a fire. When the doors to the elevator opened, he stepped in; only it was an open elevator shaft. He plunged some eighteen feet down to his death.

During the 1990s, six of the mill buildings were converted into the luxury apartments known as Clocktower Place. Through the years, residents and various maintenance and cleaning staff have experienced mysterious occurrences they just can't explain. All of the following incidents seem to occur late in the night or in the early morning hours.

If you ever visit, you might hear stories about strange things happening late at night. Lights flicker on and off by themselves, and televisions start playing with no one there to watch. You might hear or feel a presence and turn around, heart pounding, only to find . . . nothing. Or, maybe you'll hear the soft sound of a woman singing or the distant laughter of children, though the halls are empty.

One story goes that in the Phase One part of the building, there are multiple reports of a male ghost with dark hair, a thick beard, and a tall top hat. He looks like someone from the distant past, his eyes always watching, like he's in charge of the place. But before you can even blink, he's *gone*—faded into the shadows or disappearing into the walls.

And there's the little girl. She wears an old mill uniform, and her hair is in neat braids. She likes to play tricks, moving toys around and giggling when no one's looking. Children have complained about hearing her footsteps in the hall or seeing her for just a moment before she disappears around a corner. Late at night, when everything is supposed to be quiet, there have been numerous reports of her laughter and the sound of children running through the hall. But when you look, the hallway is always empty.

A couple have reported their bedroom door slamming on its own. Also, several times a mysterious large thirteen-inch boot print has appeared in their carpet after they just vacuumed it. They have also seen ghostly figures pass by in the hall. These events happen whenever the resident plays his guitar or music too loudly. To make peace, he has turned down the music.

One evening in October 2018, a gentleman (who has lived in the Phase One building for twelve years) had an experience he will never forget. He was walking back on the Water Street ramp after picking up some pizza nearby with the plan to watch a football game on television. As he was walking toward his building, he noticed a woman sitting on the park bench looking down at the river. "She was pale and had on a white long Victorian-style dress with ruffles around the neck. She had long black hair." He said he walked up to the glass doors and was fumbling with his keys to open them. He looked up, and in the reflection of the door, saw the woman standing right behind him! He quickly went through the doorway and looked back, and the woman was back at the bench. "She was sitting on the bench, and she was staring right at me. There was no physical way she could have gotten there so quickly. Now, I don't believe in this sort of thing, but I just can't explain this. It doesn't make sense, but it happened. I didn't even wait for the elevator. I ran up the stairs. It scared me so much, and I will never ever forget it."

In another part of the building, a couple had an unforgettable ghostly encounter. Late one night, they stepped into the elevator, only to be joined by a woman wearing an old dress from another time. They immediately noticed a strong, strange scent, which was "very moldy and musty," emanating from her. The couple shared how it was weird that she just stood there and seemed to ignore them. She didn't say a word, and when they asked what floor she needed, she just turned to them with a strange smile and whispered, "Sure."

The elevator doors opened, and she floated out, vanishing before their very eyes. Eek!

And then there's the bed. Imagine this: you leave your bed neatly made in the morning, but when you come back, the covers are tossed around, like someone has been sleeping there. Also, there is a light in the hallway that burns out again and again, no matter how many times it's replaced by the staff.

And then there's the constant knocking coming from inside the walls. Who could it be, and what do they want?

Some say the noises and strange happenings at Clocktower Place are just the creaks and groans of an old building. Others believe they are the ghostly reminders of the past that refuse to be forgotten. If you ever find yourself near those tall, beautiful buildings by the river, remember, you just may have someone watching you from beyond.

CHAPTER 4

The Wailing Woman on Factory Street

This sad and haunting tale passed down through the years tells of Mrs. John Goodvitch, who mourns her beloved son Adam, lost in a most tragic event in 1928 when he was just nine years old.

It all started one night when Nashua patrolman Robert Mennier spotted what he thought was a prowler. Instead, he found something far worse: a young boy's body lying in the autumn leaves. Adam died in an alley behind the Main Street Methodist Church, and the news devastated his family and shook the whole city. According to an article in *The Nashua Telegraph*, "There was revealed what police today believe to be the most unusual juvenile murder in the criminal annals of the city and state."

The story goes that Adam, along with two other boys, had formed a secret gang, inspired by crime stories and movies they loved. The three boys had committed a string of small thefts around town. Then, things took a terrible twist. After an argument, Adam's supposed friends turned against him, and Adam was killed for confessing and revealing their crimes to the police.

The Goodvitch family lived in a small apartment on the top floor of a building on Factory Street. Adam was an only child and had been in the third grade. Mrs. Goodvitch's heart-wrenching cries were said to haunt the street, a sad reminder of the tragic loss of her son.

On dark October nights, especially around the 24th, you may still hear the sorrowful cries that haunted Factory Street. This tragic story is a sad lesson and warning of how crime leads to the worst loss imaginable.

Be careful whom you choose for friends.

CHAPTER 5

The Haunted Tavern

Nashua residents and visitors have been enjoying the delicious food and spirits of the Fody's Great American Tavern since 2004, but the ghosts have been haunting the building for more than a century.

According to the history of the tavern, formerly known as the Greeley building, it was built in 1833 by three brothers—Ezekiel, Joseph, and Alfred Greeley—and is actually the oldest brick building in Nashua.

Strangely, the building was moved to make

room for the Hunt Memorial Building. After its relocation in 1885, the building played several key roles in Nashua's evolving downtown landscape. It eventually became the Tavern Hotel under the ownership of Police Commissioner J. Howard Giles.

The hotel flourished in the location of Railroad Square, attracting a steady flow of visitors who would arrive by train to work or shop in the stores downtown. Over the years, the building has been an important place in Nashua's history. At different times it served as the city hall, a meeting house, a church, a store, a morgue, and a pool hall.

The Historical Society of Nashua says that in the 1960s, people claimed the building became a place where illegal activities happened. It was told to me that the building was once a brothel, and it even says so in the restaurant's history. (Although there are no resources to prove it.) Still, stories like this—and spooky tales—have been passed down by local people over the years.

In 2004, Fody's Great American Tavern took over and restored the building, creating a bustling spot for social gatherings—and it seems some ghostly guests may enjoy those gatherings, too! Staff have reported strange occurrences, such as unexplained footsteps, flickering lights, and the feeling of being watched.

One waitress shared that the water in the bathroom mysteriously turns on by itself. Staff have reported hearing banging from upstairs, but no one is up there.

"It's definitely haunted," one local resident shared. "But that just adds to the place."

Given the building's long, rich history, it's easy to imagine why stories of ghosts have emerged through the years. Overall, the ghosts seem happy to keep to themselves, quietly lingering in the background. They seem to be pleased with how the staff has honored the history and spirit of the old tavern. The spirits of the tavern are always watching from the shadows while customers enjoy their hearty meals in front of that old, cozy fireplace. So, mind your manners!

CHAPTER 6

The Ghosts of the Hunt Community Home

The Hunt Community Home was built way back in 1896 and has been a place of care for older people in the community for many years. Over time, it has grown into a beautiful retirement and senior living community (where my own grandparents resided), so people can get help and support as they grow older. And with such a long history, there are a few ghost stories in this building.

Residents have reported hearing orchestra music playing in the middle of the night. Staff have seen lights flicker, shadow figures, and the feelings that they weren't alone. And, through the years, the ghosts have even baffled security and local police!

One story happened during a summer night in the early 1980s, when two Nashua police officers were called to the old John Hunt building while it was being renovated. There was a spooky tunnel that connected it to the nearby Mary Hunt building. A security guard at the Mary Hunt building had heard strange noises on the speaker of a party going on in the empty John Hunt building. He told the officers it sounded like laughter, clinking glasses, and music, and he thought it might be a group of kids sneaking in to have fun.

Curious and annoyed, the two officers and the security guard headed through the dark tunnel to investigate. But when they got to the John Hunt building, everything was silent. Flashlights in hand, they checked every floor. The building was old and creepy, especially the attic,

which had dusty old wheelchairs and rusty bed frames. One of the officers described it as if the place hadn't been touched for years. They found nothing—not a single person.

After searching the entire building, they returned to the security office. But as soon as they got back, they heard the party noises again through the speaker. They heard the same laughter, talking, and clinking glasses! Startled, they rushed back through the tunnel to the John Hunt building, but once again, everything was quiet. Then, as they stood at the bottom of the stairs, a playing card floated down from the air, landing at one of the officer's feet. It was the four of clubs!

They dashed up the stairs, expecting to find someone, but there was no one. The building was completely empty. When they returned to the bottom of the stairs, they noticed something even stranger: a single set of wet footprints, but no sign of where they came from.

One officer turned to the security guard and said, "There's nothing we can do to help you with this. Whoever, or whatever was here is gone." Later, the officers agreed to keep the story to themselves, figuring no one would believe them anyway. And to this day, the mysterious experiences of that night are remembered!

Here's another haunted story about the Hunt Home!

An old security officer who worked at the Hunt Community shared a chilling story. One night, as he was doing his rounds, he stopped at a large mirror in the hallway. He adjusted his hat, glanced at his reflection, and kept walking. From behind him, a nurse called out, "Tell your friend he can't go down there!"

Puzzled, the security officer turned to the nurse and asked, "Who are you talking about?" She pointed down the hall and said, "The man in the chef outfit with the black-and-white checkered pants. He can't go down there."

The officer froze. "No one's with me," he replied. He quickly looked around, but the hallway was empty. Even in the mirror, it had just been him. There was no chef, no one else. The air felt colder, and he got the creeps every night after that. That eerie encounter haunted him for years!

Stories like these have become a part of the charm and history of what makes the building so special. Some believe the friendly ghosts are simply watching over the residents and staff, making sure everyone is cared for and safe . . . and remembered.

Hunt Community Home

CHAPTER 7

The Spirit of Martha's Exchange Restaurant & Brewery

On Main Street stands one of the most beloved historic spots in the city, Martha's Exchange Restaurant and Brewery. For many years, families and friends have dined here to celebrate and enjoy some of the most delicious food and spirits around. But there's something else at Martha's, something not everyone knows about—a ghost!

Martha's Exchange Restaurant and Brewery is a strong fixture in Nashua's historic downtown district, being in close proximity to the former

Nashua Mill buildings, The Nashua Telegraph Building, and the city's government offices. The building has endured the tests of time, and it even survived a fire that nearly destroyed the building one bitter cold night in February of 1930.

As the *Telegraph* reported at the time, "The fire was one of the most disastrous this city has witnessed in some years and in spite of the biting cold weather hundreds of persons lined the streets to watch the fire."

According to the restaurant's history, Martha's Exchange Restaurant started many years ago with a woman named Katherine who came all the way from Greece to Nashua. In 1936, Katherine opened the original Martha's Sweet Shoppe, named after a popular candy of the time called "Martha Washington Candy." Back then, the store was just a small space—much smaller than what you see today. Now, it is four stories and a special place for parties of all sizes to enjoy.

In 1944, Katherine's nephew, James Fokas (or Mitch, as most people called him), returned from World War II and took over the candy shop.

He made it bigger and added a luncheonette.

In 1985, Bill Fokas took over the family business and transformed the small luncheonette and candy shop into a much larger restaurant, bar, and function center. Bill added Nashua's first microbrewery and brought in a bar from (a notorious gangster) Al Capone's old speakeasies, adding a bit of mystery to the restaurant's charm!

Through good times and bad, Martha's Exchange has remained at the heart of Nashua and a family tradition, offering comfort, connection, and delicious meals for all who visit. And, through the years, one thing has remained constant—the presence of Katherine, who founded the original sweet shop. Some believe her ghost still watches over Martha's Exchange, ensuring the family legacy lives on.

Several staff members have reported seeing her in the restaurant, as if quietly checking in on things. Staff also often feel as if someone is watching them on the third floor, and many have sensed this same invisible presence while in the basement.

Most recently, the seven-year-old daughter of a staff member spotted Katherine in the Sweet Shoppe, describing her as a friendly figure with a warm smile. When the waitress asked her daughter who she was talking to, the little girl replied, "The nice old lady." But when the staff members looked, no one was there. She had disappeared.

After all these years, the spirit of Martha's lives on. Some say, quite literally! Some staff also believe the spirits of the family continue to watch over their beloved restaurant from beyond. If you go, make sure you try their delicious chocolate!

CHAPTER 8

The Foundry Specter

This ghostly tale comes from the archives of *The Nashua Telegraph* newspaper. According to an article published on January 13th, 1873, there was a ghost reported at the old Williams Foundry.

Back in the 1800s, this foundry was a big workshop where workers melted metal and shaped it into useful things like tools, parts for machines, and even parts of buildings. These metalworkers would heat the metal until it was so hot it turned into a liquid, then pour it into molds to make the right shapes. Also, working at the foundry was a very grueling job. Workers had to carry heavy, boiling-hot pots of melted metal, and if they spilled even a little, it could cause a fire or severely burn someone. Foundries were dangerous because the metal was so hot. It was also hard to breathe because the air filled with dust and smoke. And there were loud, noisy machines that could be risky to work around if people weren't careful.

According to the old *Telegraph* article, a woman known as Mrs. Grundy shared a rumor that the foundry was haunted by the ghosts of those poor lost souls. It is said that one night a ghost appeared to a watchman. "He spoke no word nor did he explain his mission."

The sight of the specter filled the watchman with terror and dismay. He fled and ran to his house. "There was no sleep, no rest, no relief from terror until dawn of day." Mrs. Grundy said.

Apparently, he truly believed the spirit had returned from the grave. Perhaps the watchman's imagination got the best of him, or maybe he just had a bad night. Who knows? Maybe late at night, the ghost of the foundry still waits . . . for you!

CHAPTER 9

The Ghost in the Café

The staff at the Riverwalk Bakery & Café in Nashua love serving coffee and making delicious pastries, breakfast, and lunch for their customers. However, there is one customer that continues to mystify them: a ghost!

In a historic old building in Railroad Square, the owners, Rachel and Mike, took over the café in April 2022 and immediately expanded and started renovations. During these renovations, they realized that they had a ghost watching over them. Working hard to improve the place, they found themselves working eighteen to twenty hours a day and were often at the café late at night. During this time, they would often feel like they weren't alone. They had the eerie feeling that someone was watching over them, and sometimes unexplainable things would happen.

One night, Rachel and Mike were heading out to see a movie with friends. They turned on the security alarms, locked all the doors, and left the café completely silent. But when they returned at the end of the night, they found the stereo blasting music at full volume! In fact, Rachel and Mike believe that their ghost seems to really love music. The stereo often turns on all by itself, with the volume cranked way up. Perhaps their invisible housemate likes to have dance parties when they're away?

That isn't all! Once, Rachel went into the kitchen and found all the food coloring bottles she keeps in a basket lined up neatly on the floor. Rachel has occasionally caught glimpses of movement out of the corner of her eye and spotted a shadowy figure. On another evening, Rachel,

Mike, and her mother were the only ones in the building. Rachel's mother went to use the restroom and locked the door behind her. The door handle began to rattle and move like someone was trying to open the door. When Rachel's mother came out, she asked Rachel and Mike why they'd done that, but they did not know what she was talking about. They had not touched the door.

Another time, they witnessed a door close on its own. When they later reviewed the security cameras, they clearly heard a man's voice say, "Get away." (They actually showed me the recording, and I heard the voice, too.)

Rachel feels certain the ghost is a man with a strong presence. She believes he watches over the café like a guardian, protecting it from harm. "Sometimes there are nights when the café feels empty, and then there are nights when you definitely know you are not alone.

The air will feel weird, and the music will kick in," Rachel said.

Despite the music and odd encounters, Rachel and Mike believe the ghost is friendly and feels at home. Now that renovations are complete, they say the spooky activity has calmed down for the most part. Even though sometimes, late at night, the ghost still likes to listen to his tunes.

Riverwalk Bakery & Café

CHAPTER 10

The Haunted Bridge

On the north side of the city, as you head towards the town of Hudson, is an old railroad trestle bridge nicknamed "The Black Bridge" because of the tragedies that have happened there over the years.

In 1954, a train called the "Red Wing" jumped the tracks in Nashua, killing one passenger, Mrs. Mary Buckley, and injuring many others.

Six years later, another train crash happened not far from there. In 1960, a terrible accident happened when a train hit a truck carrying propane gas. According to the *Telegraph*, six people were killed. Their names were Robert Wrenn, his wife Patricia, their children Jennifer (one month old) and Christopher (eighteen months), train conductor Vaughn Talbot, and John Wilder.

Sadly, there have also been drug or mental health-related deaths that police have been called to over the years.

Supposedly, some locals claim to have heard the ghostly voices of children laughing and seen shadows roaming along the riverbank after dusk. Are these the poor souls of those who have drowned, or the spirits of those lost in the battles long ago? We may never know. Despite having a spooky and tragic past, it is a peaceful place to walk and kayak. Just don't go there after sunset.

CHAPTER 11

The Ghost on the Stairs

A long time ago, there was a place in Nashua called the Poor Farm, where people who were sick or didn't have a home could go to live. It opened in 1858 on Fairway Street, and for many years, people who couldn't care for themselves lived there and did chores on the farm. But by 1908, the Poor Farm closed, and the city began offering other ways to help people.

In 1915, a group of local businessmen bought the land where the Poor Farm once stood. They wanted to make a place where people could play sports, make friends, and have fun. They turned the old farm into the Nashua Country Club, and over time, it grew into a big, fancy place that lots of people respect today.

But some say the past still lingers there.

Late at night, when most people have gone home, some workers at the country club have seen strange things. There's a story about a ghostly woman in a white wedding dress. She walks quietly down the stairs or sits in a chair near the back of the building. Some local people claim to have seen her with two ghostly children by her side.

Others report sightings of another spectral woman in a brown dress, with a chatelaine (a woman's belt chain with tiny tools such as keys, a pen, scissors, a thimble, a needle book, a whistle, and glasses) hanging from around her waist as she charges down the stairs. She walks with purpose, as if she is inspecting the halls.

Some wonder if she was the woman who helped run the old Poor Farm so many years ago. Is she still making sure everyone has what they need?

Even spookier are the times when workers have reported hearing voices and laughter of children echoing through the halls—but when they go to look, no one is there. Sometimes, lights flicker on and off, doors open by themselves, and objects appear to move on their own.

No one really knows who these ghosts are, but perhaps they remain because they are happiest here.

CHAPTER 12

The Legend of Mine Falls

Mine Falls Park is a beautiful 325-acre forested park with wonderful trails and sports fields for all to enjoy. The park sits between the Nashua River and the Mill Pond canal. It is a favorite spot for people who love nature and is considered a gem of the city. The park is so special that it's part of the New Hampshire Heritage Trail, and the Nashua Millyard is listed on the National Register of Historic Places.

But did you know it's also a place with a mysterious past?

According to local history, the name "Mine Falls" comes from the 1700s. Back then, people believed there was lead hidden in the land near the falls. Even though they didn't find much, the name stuck. Later, in the early 1800s, the Nashua River was used to power huge mills that helped build the city. Workers dug a three-mile-long canal using only shovels and mules! Talk about hard labor!

Today, you can still see the old gatehouse near the falls. It was built in 1886. Mine Falls is more than just a park; it's also a fascinating place where history and mystery meet the ghosts of the past.

When the sun goes down and the park becomes quiet, some say the spirits of the workers who built the canal and searched for treasure still roam the land. They wander down the trails, just as they did long ago. Others have seen strange shadows moving near the water. Could they be the ghosts of the old mill and canal workers, watching over the park they helped create? Or, are they watching over their treasure?

Here is a Nashua tale of treasure that has survived through the years, thanks to the old stories from the author Edward E. Parker.

A long time ago, a man named Hezekiah Usher was given some small islands at the base of what is now known as Mine Falls in Nashua. There were rumors that hidden treasures lay beneath the land.

According to the story, Hezekiah Usher was a man with big dreams and ideas. Like many explorers of the time, he had heard stories of places filled with gold and silver, and he thought New England might have hidden riches, too. There was also a legend whispered by the Indigenous tribes about a magical gem called the "Great Carbuncle," which was said to sparkle on the highest mountains, where no one dared to go because it was protected by spirits. The folklore also inspired the author Nathaniel Hawthorne to write a story about the "Great Carbuncle" in 1835.

Usher was so inspired that he dug into the ground and found some lead and iron, but there wasn't much of it. Eventually, he gave up, and his search for the treasure ended.

Legend has it that on quiet nights, you may hear the sounds of digging from the ghostly canal workers, or the miners still searching for the riches Usher dreamed so much about. And as you walk down the paths at sunset or in the early morning, you might even catch a glimpse of glowing lights flickering between the trees. Be warned . . . it may be wise not to follow them.

CHAPTER 13

The Haunt

Would you ever buy a house if it was haunted? This is an odd tale of a haunted house that comes from old articles in the *Telegraph* and *Cabinet Press* newspapers and a volunteer from the Historical Society who grew up near the home.

The story of "The Haunt" began around 1740, when the saltbox farmhouse was built on the Nashua River. The story goes that an old sailor who worked on the farm kept his knife, money, and other valuables under his pillow. One night, his coworkers murdered him in his bed for his treasure. Soon after, people claimed the sailor's ghost haunted the house in search of his lost treasure. Supposedly, his ghost would come up in a haze from out of the fireplace at eight o'clock at night and then disappear.

Over the years, these ghostly tales attracted so much interest that several newspapers published them. In 1896, William E. Spalding, a Boston financier and antique dealer, admired the home while boating on the river. After hearing about the spooky tales, he went to explore the house. As he approached the building, he saw three flashes of light, and, when he stepped inside with a friend, a powerful gust of wind blew through the room, snuffing out their candles. Then, without warning, bricks mysteriously began to fall from the roof! But Spalding wasn't scared. In fact, he liked the house so much that he bought it, and had it moved to where it is today.

Through the years, the home was renovated and housed many historical treasures. If those old walls could talk, just imagine the stories they would tell!

CHAPTER 14

The North End Specter

In Nashua, there's an old house in the north end right near Holman Stadium that has a very haunted history. It's a large, two-story home with a sad past. Long ago, a mother and her son passed away there from an illness. Later, residents of the house claimed to hear strange, unexplainable noises. Some people think the spirits of the mother and son still live in the house. Others believe there must be a logical explanation for the strange noises. But so far, no one has solved the mystery of the eerie sounds.

During the late 1800s, a family moved into the house, and odd things happened right away. An article published in *The Nashua Telegraph* on November 16, 1880, described the family's eerie experiences. Their doorbell would ring, but they'd open the door to find no one there. They heard footsteps echoing through the house, yet the halls remained empty. One night, loud banging noises from the kitchen woke everyone up—it sounded like someone was moving pots and pans around. But when the family rushed downstairs to check, nothing was out of place. Each night, the noises continued. They would hear groaning, footsteps, and rattling stove covers. At times, the family felt a strange pressure, as if someone was pushing past them. Frightened, they soon moved out, leaving behind the mystery of the haunted house.

"It is told that the room in which the woman died has been lighted an hour at a time, after midnight, that forms have been seen and seances held and much more that seems to make the sum total of a haunted house," the *Telegraph* stated.

People still talk about the house to this day! Do you think the ghosts also talk about *them*?

CHAPTER 15

The Country Tavern

No collection of Nashua's ghost stories would be complete without this famous and spooky old tale. Where a gas station now sits on Amherst Street today, there was a haunted spot known as the Country Tavern. Once a farmhouse that dated back to the 1700s, this colonial home held a tragic story of jealousy and death.

According to Nashua folklore and articles in the *Nashua Telegraph*, the story goes that a man named Captain Ford built the house in 1741, but it was primarily his much younger wife, Elizabeth, who lived there. Captain Ford was often away at sea for long stretches, leaving Elizabeth all alone. After one particularly long voyage, the captain returned to a shocking surprise: Elizabeth had given birth to a baby. Knowing he had been gone for over a year, Captain Ford realized the baby could not be his. Consumed by jealousy and a terrible temper, he did the unthinkable and took the baby's life. When Elizabeth discovered what her husband had done, she sought revenge. However, Captain Ford was stronger. He killed Elizabeth and threw her body into the well behind the house.

As time passed, the tavern became famous for the heartbroken ghost who mourned her baby. Over the years, employees reported strange things. Utensils and dishes would sometimes move on their own, and an eerie presence seemed to watch them as they worked. One of the owners would hear the ghost rattling around late at night when she was doing the books alone. When she drove away, she would often see a face gazing at her from a window. Though the building was later torn down and a gas station built in its place, people still talk about this ghost story.

CHAPTER 16

The Ghosts of the Hassell Family

Between Hassell Brook Road and Almont Street, there is a small, wooded path that holds a tragic tale. Right in the middle of the path stands a large rock that is a memorial for a family from long ago. If you visit this path, you will see a plaque on the rock. It tells the story of a terrible event that happened over 300 years ago, on September 2, 1691.

The story goes that during this early time, there was great tension between the new settlers and the Indigenous people who had lived on the land for many generations. On that day, Joseph Hassell, his wife Anna, their son Benjamin, and a friend who was visiting named Mary Marks lost their lives when their home was attacked and burned to the ground.

This memorial rock marks the place where the family's home once stood. It says that Joseph, Anna, Benjamin, and Mary are buried right there, where they died.

According to local legend, this spot is still haunted. And sometimes, on stormy autumn nights—if you listen carefully—you may hear their cries in the howling wind.

CHAPTER 17

The Abbot-Spalding House

The Abbot-Spalding House sits at the top of Main Street and is a special place where visitors can learn about Nashua's rich history. According to the Nashua Historical Society, this grand house once belonged to the Honorable Daniel Abbot, a man known as the "Father of Nashua." He was a lawyer, leader, and speaker and played a big role in shaping Nashua's early days. Most importantly, Daniel Abbot founded the Nashua Manufacturing Company. He was the first owner of the house, which today is a treasured part of the Nashua

Historical Society. Daniel Abbot bought the land for $300 around 1802, and he hired a man named John Lund to build this beautiful colonial-style home. Daniel Abbot lived in the house until he passed away on December 3, 1853.

William Edward Spalding, the fourth owner of the house, was very involved in Nashua's community. He served as vice president of the

The Abbot-Spalding House

First National Bank, represented his ward, was city treasurer, and participated in many city organizations. He was also an assistant to New Hampshire Governor Charles Sawyer from 1887 to 1889. William Spalding loved history and eventually started his own antique business. (Read about him in Chapter 13: The Haunt.) His daughter, Sylvia, sold the house to the Nashua Historical Society in 1978, but she continued to live there for the rest of her life. When Sylvia passed away in 1984, she left the house and everything inside to the Nashua Historical Society.

You can visit the Abbot-Spalding House by appointment or during special days when the house is open for events. And who knows? If you visit, you might just feel their community spirit, too.

CHAPTER 18

The Ghost of West Pearl Street

West Pearl Street has been a busy place for a long time. Long ago, horses and carriages clattered down the road, and there were people walking to the mills, shops, or staying at the grand Tremont House hotel. There was also a brick schoolhouse and a market store. The street was one of the first built in Nashua in the early 1800s. And with all this history comes a few mysteries . . .

Now the busy street holds several businesses: a flower shop, a tattoo parlor, a café, a magical herbal shop, a barber, a wallpaper store, several restaurants and a couple apartment buildings. One old apartment building has been here since the 1800s and some of the residents have had a few ghostly encounters.

One night, a woman who lived on the second floor heard someone walking up the stairs and right past her door. *Step . . . step . . . step . . .*

She thought it was her neighbor coming home, so she opened her door to say hello.

But no one was there. The hall was empty.

She listened. Nothing. Then she got goose bumps and had the feeling she was being watched. Shaking her head, she closed the door.

But there is more.

Another night, she was woken up by a loud *BANG!* Then there was the sound of furniture scraping across the floor above her. *SCRRRRAPE! THUMP!*

Puzzled because no one lived in the apartment above her, she grabbed a flashlight and hurried upstairs. Just as she reached the landing, the neighbors across from the empty apartment peeked out. They were a young couple who had lived there for a few months.

"Do you hear it, too?" they whispered in fear.

She nodded. Together, they slowly tiptoed to

the door and pressed their ears closely against it to listen.

Shuffle . . . scrape . . . knock . . .

They knocked back.

Silence. They knocked again.

Nothing.

They decided they would ask their landlord.

The next morning, they hurried to tell Vivian Walker, the landlord who was in her dress shop downstairs.

"Has anyone moved into the third-floor apartment?" they asked.

Vivian frowned. "No, that apartment is empty."

"Well, someone is up there!" they insisted.

Vivian grabbed her keys, and together they climbed the stairs to the third floor. She turned the key and pushed open the door.

Inside, the apartment was empty and quiet. No furniture. No sign that anyone had been there at all. But for several nights, the tenants would hear the mysterious noises coming from that apartment for about a week. And then, it just stopped.

And that wasn't even the strangest part of the building's history. In the basement, there's a tunnel that connects to other buildings and businesses. Some say the tunnels were used long ago, maybe for secret meetings. But in one of the connected basements . . . there is something very odd. There is a *grave.*

Yep. There is a gravestone, and it says "Thomas." No one knows for sure who is buried there. Some think it might belong to a worker from the old nearby mills, or maybe it is the ghost of a former guest at the Tremont House.

Three of the shops have had employees report a male ghostly presence. Those who have experienced it think he just does not want to leave. He still lingers, protecting the old buildings and those inside . . . and he hopes you will shop in downtown Nashua, especially on West Pearl Street.

Part 2: Graves from the Past

Gravestone of Walter Gilson

"It was as if nature had fixed her sign of desolation on this spot, warning off all human wanderers from it as from a ruin where restless spirits might still haunt, and warn the living from their unblessed graves."

— *The House of the Seven Gables* by Nathaniel Hawthorne (1851)

There is just something so mysterious and intriguing about cemeteries. Exploring the local cemeteries can offer a glimpse into the community's history and the lives of the settlers from the past. One can't help but notice the various old stones and dates and wonder about their lives so many years ago. The three oldest burial locations in the city of Nashua are the Old South Burying Ground and Gilson Cemetery, as well as a memorial rock at Greeley Park. If you should visit, please be respectful of these final resting places, gravestones, and monuments. After all . . . you never know whose rest you may be disturbing.

Old South Burying Ground and Schoolhouse

CHAPTER 19

Old South Burying Ground

On Daniel Webster Highway stands the Old South Burying Ground, the oldest cemetery in Nashua, once part of Dunstable. Dating back to 1687, this cemetery holds the graves of the city's earliest settlers.

According to Jane Flythe's book *God's Acre: A History of the Old South Burial Ground*, among the graves rest Nashua's first two ministers, soldiers from the Indian and French wars, the Revolutionary War, and the War of 1812. Many of these early settlers were well known for their influence during colonial times.

Right next to the cemetery, you will also find the Suburban Schoolhouse No. 1, built in 1871. It was placed there because the land was cheap and maybe because the neighbors weren't expected to disturb them . . . or complain of being disturbed.

Some locals claim to have experienced a strange phenomenon of glimpsing a shadowy figure floating among the graves. Could it be a spirit watching over the brave pioneers who rest here? If you go, please be respectful of those who are buried in this historic cemetery.

CHAPTER

20

Gilson Road Cemetery

On the outskirts of Nashua is a small, humble graveyard surrounded by a rock wall and woods called Gilson Road Cemetery. It is named after the John Gilson family, who were the first settlers. It is rumored to be very haunted, and it is a popular spot for ghost enthusiasts and history buffs. This place has reports of ghostly voices, shadowy figures, and feelings of being pushed by ice-cold hands.

One story told to me by a local fireman was that if you look through the hole on one of the graves, you will see the spirits of the warriors from long ago staring back at you from along the rock wall. This gravestone is of the young Walter Gilson, who died at only five years old on August 28, 1811. In the middle of the stone, there's a strange hole, about an inch wide, drilled right through. No one knows why the hole is there, but it adds a spooky touch to the story of this long-ago resting place.

There are also stories of the ghostly figure of the little boy running through the cemetery and on the road. Many have also claimed to have seen a mysterious woman in white, sadly wandering among the infant graves and drifting away into the shadows.

This small cemetery is certainly a spooky place to see, with its graves dating back to the 1700s. Whatever you do, don't go at night, or you may be followed home by a ghost . . . or the police.

CHAPTER 21

Greeley Park Memorial Rock

Tucked away on the eastern side of the beautiful Greeley Park and surrounded by trees is a walkway that leads to a large boulder. Long ago, this stone was placed to memorialize the sacred spot where the first settlers in the north end of Nashua were buried.

Over time, the graves of these brave pioneers vanished, worn away by so many years of wind and harsh weather. Now, the only thing left to remember these pioneers is this boulder, standing silently where their resting place once was. On quiet nights, you might just feel the presence of those brave early settlers who helped build Nashua so very long ago. If anything, they must be proud of how far the city has come after all these years.

Greeley Park Memorial Rock

CHAPTER 22

The Graves Under the School

In 1916, a most creepy discovery was made at the Spring Street Grammar School. An article published on July 12, 1916, in *the Nashua Telegraph* reported that a man named Albert Lavoie, who was helping dig at the school, unearthed an old skeleton! Well, when Mr. Lavoie realized what he'd found, he supposedly set a record for jumping backward in terror! Wouldn't you?

Oddly, the skeleton wasn't even in a casket. It was discovered underground, dressed in pieces of an old uniform with brass buttons that still shone brightly. High leather boots, very old-fashioned and unusual, were found with leg bones inside.

According to the story, the land where the school stood actually used to be a cemetery! In 1872, most of the graves were moved to Woodlawn Cemetery on West Hollis Street, but somehow, this soldier had been mistakenly forgotten.

After the grim discovery, the remains were respectfully placed in a coffin and finally laid to rest at Woodlawn Cemetery.

However, a ghost seemed to have made itself right at home in the school.

Many believed this because of the strange things that started to happen at the school. Sometimes, the toilets would suddenly flush on their own,

echoing down empty hallways. Water fountains burst to life without anyone pressing the button. Students would watch in amazement as pencil sharpeners cranked and turned all on their own, as if by an invisible hand. And just when things couldn't get any spookier, classroom lights would flicker and dim mysteriously, as if someone—or *something*—was playing with the switches.

Today, the school is long gone, and we may never know the truth about these otherworldly happenings. Where ghostly footsteps once echoed, the Hillsborough County Superior Courthouse now stands. But who knows? Perhaps the ghosts of the former Spring Street School are still lurking, in search of their favorite teacher.

Part 3:

Abenaki Legends & Ghostly Folklore

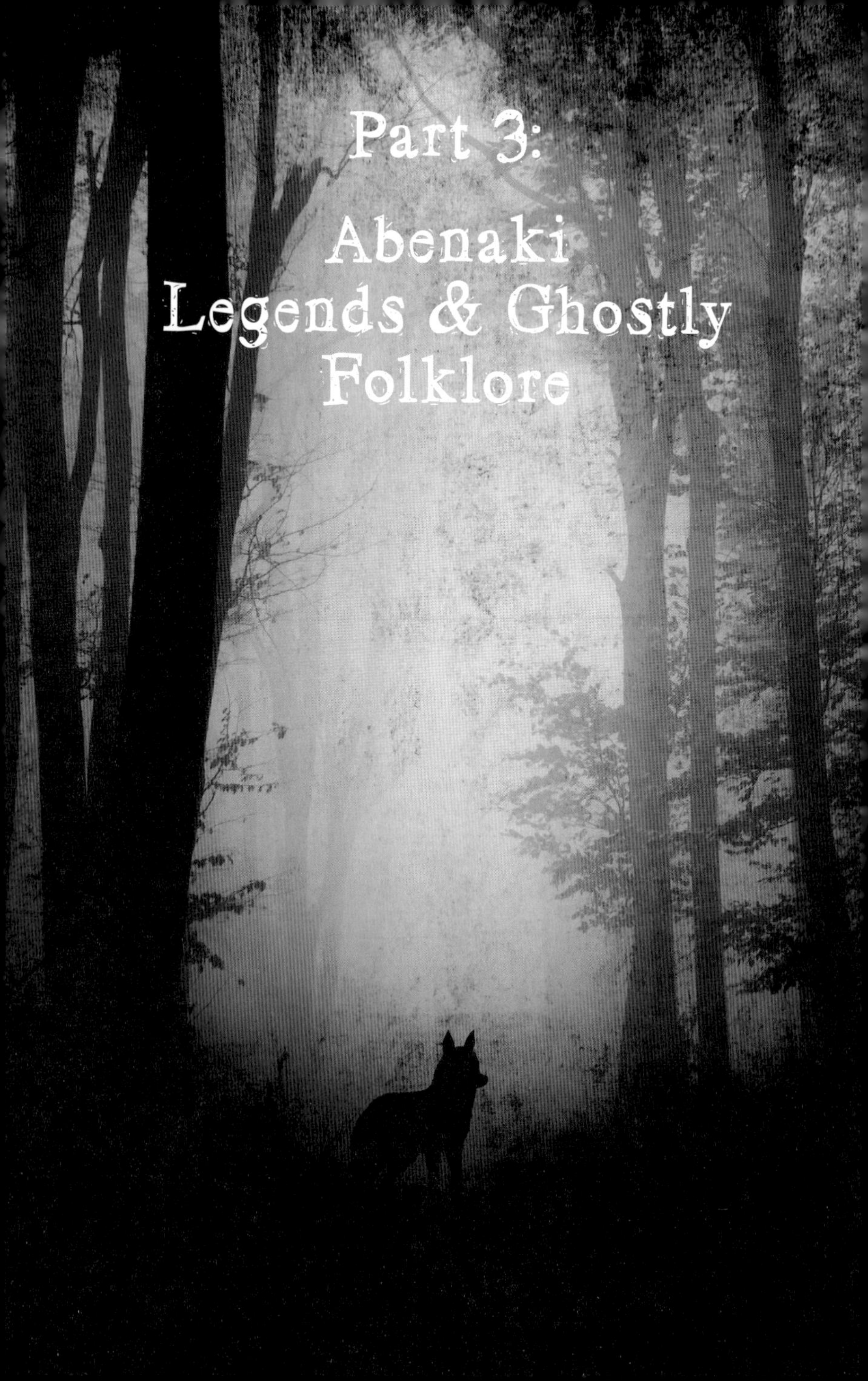

Folklore from the Abenaki group of the Pennacook tribe who once resided in the area of Nashua is important to include and remember in the history of the city. They may have left long ago, but their spirits linger along the rivers and forests.

According to the book *New Hampshire, A Guide to the Granite State*, the Abenaki believed in spirits. The name for spirit was Manitou, and it "was given to a spirit which might be good or evil." Long, long ago, lived the Abenaki people, known as the "Dawn Land People" or the "People of the Dawn." As shared in the book *Keepers of the Night* by Michael J. Caduto and Joseph Bruchac, the stories from the tribes shared the lives and their beliefs in the spirits of the animals and elements. Through the art of storytelling, they would often weave a tale by firelight to entertain and teach their children. Perhaps you will learn the lessons from their stories, too.

CHAPTER 23

The Spirit of the Raccoon

According to Abenaki legend, Azeban is a mischievous spirit creature who takes the shape of a raccoon. Azeban is pronounced ah-zuh-bahn. He often behaves foolishly and causes trouble for others, but he is not all bad. However, he is obsessed with food, so if you are missing any food or camping items, it may be Azeban! So watch your stuff! He just might steal it!

This sly creature really likes sneaking food and playing tricks to get food in the forest. On autumn nights, as the moon shines bright, Azeban may try to spook those hanging out in the woods. Always hungry, he will hide in the shadows and wait for the perfect opportunity to steal food.

One young couple from the local tribe had made their camp in the nearby woods. They made a small fire to cook their meal. Watching from a distance, Azeban slowly tiptoed through the trees, making spooky scratching noises and loud crunching footsteps in the leaves. The couple stopped eating and froze in terror as they listened to the loud noises growing closer and closer and closer. They watched this strange shadow of a creature appear. Soon, they realized the "ghost" was none other than Azeban, who was trying to sneak their supper away from them!

Laughing, they chased the Azeban away into the night. "I will be back!" he squeaked!

Azeban teaches us to keep our sense of humor, but always keep an eye out. You never know what is going to happen next! Remember, don't leave your food out. Pick up your trash, and keep Mine Falls clean for all to enjoy.

If you don't, Azeban will be sure to remind you!

CHAPTER

24

The Spirit of the Squirrel

Miko takes on the spirit of the squirrel in Abenaki legends. Pronounced mee-ko.

Miko, the squirrel, has keen eyes and a bushy tail. Miko always watches over the forest, high in the trees of Mine Falls. He darts from branch to branch, chattering loudly.

It is important to listen to his warnings: “Be careful! The forest is not always what it seems!”

Though Miko is often a troublemaker who likes to hit you with his acorns, he knows things, and the animals listen to his advice.

Please know that the forest, while beautiful, can be full of hidden dangers.

Pay attention and listen to your surroundings. There are many signs to guide you, including Miko! Also, if you go into the woods, be respectful of this special place.

Remember, the spirit of Miko is watching you, always! If you see him, thank him for watching over the forest and keeping you safe.

CHAPTER 25

A Terrifying Abenaki Ghost Witch Story

This final terrifying old tale is inspired from the translated Abenaki tale by Beulah Tahamont to historians Laura Redish and Lewis Orrin. It is the tale of the Skadegamutc and is pronounced "Skuh-dak-uh-mooch."

Many, many moons ago, the old "witch" passed away in the local woods, and his people buried him in a special way. They laid him to rest up in the branches of a tall tree in a grove along the Merrimack River.

After many years, a man and his wife from the tribe were walking through the woods of the white birches looking for a place to rest. They came across the burial grove, not knowing its secrets, and decided to camp there. They built a fire and cooked their meal.

After dinner, the wife looked up and noticed long, dark shapes hanging in the tree branches.

"What are those?" she asked as she watched the shadows sway in the wind.

"They're just the bones of those who passed long ago," her husband replied. "I'm tired."

"I don't like this place," the wife whispered. "I think we should leave."

"No. I need my rest," her husband replied.

"I am scared. I think we should stay awake all night. Please." She begged.

But her husband would not listen to his wife, and he soon fell asleep and began to snore.

However, the wife found it impossible to sleep. She watched the shadows sway back and forth and listened to the wind and the sounds of the leaves crunching around her. Then, from the corner of her eye, she saw a shadow slowly crawl down a tree. Was her mind playing tricks on her?

As the fire began to burn out, the wife heard another strange sound. It was a soft, eerie noise just like an animal chewing and sucking on a bone. She curled up very small and closed her eyes tight. Terrified, she kept very still. She was too scared to move, listening to the awful sound go on and on in the dark. It went on all night, and the horrible sound got louder and louder.

By dawn, the horrible sound finally stopped. She slowly reached over to wake her husband, but he did not stir. She shook him harder, only to find that he wasn't asleep. His arm felt so terribly cold. He was dead! His side had been gnawed away, and there was a gaping hole where his heart should be.

Horrified, the woman ran as fast as she could down the path along the river. Finally, she found the nearby tribe. She sobbed as she told the tribe what had happened to her husband, and she begged them for help. Dubious, they agreed to return to the grove with her and see for themselves.

When they arrived, they found the man lying

on the ground just as she had said. He was beneath the tree where the witch had been buried. The strongest men of the group carefully brought the witch's body down from the branches and unwrapped it. To their horror, the dead witch's grin was covered in dark red blood!

The tribe held another ceremony to burn the bodies of the witch and the husband, so they would not hunger. They are both at peace.

The lesson of the story, dear children of Nashua, is to listen to your parents and never go into the forest alone at night. Be very careful in the woods!

(And, husbands, it would be very wise to listen to your wife.)

A Ghostly Goodbye

Thank you so much for reading these tales about Nashua. I graduated from Nashua High School and have so many fond memories living in this city. I hope you will try your hand at telling some of these stories or sharing your own stories with others. Storytelling is a fun way to connect, build on communication skills, and encourage imagination. It is a way to share and discuss your thoughts and beliefs with others. Telling historic and ghostly tales is one way you can help keep the past alive and inspire a love for learning. You can learn more great stories from our history by joining the Historical Society and visiting your local library.

And there, I hope you will realize, anything is possible.

Scrolls in the New Hampshire State Archives

Acknowledgements

I am very grateful to my editor, Jessica Rothenberg, and the team at Arcadia Children's Books for making this book possible. I am grateful to my friend Mike Koutrobis for writing the foreword and for bringing laughter and joy to so many. I am also thankful to my friend Lisa Starnes for helping me edit my book. I am sincerely grateful to the Nashua Historical Society, their helpful volunteers such as Mary Foran, Beth McCarthy, Alan Manoian, and Dean Shalhoup, who help protect and share the history of Nashua. I appreciate the Nashua Public Library reference librarians Julie Andrews, Julie Rosier, and the library staff who helped me with the microfiche and gave me access to the Hunt Room. Thank you to dedicated historians such as Justin Ober, Ashley Miller, Yvette Toledo, and Dianna

Wimpey at the NH State Archives. Thank you to Craig Michaud (for his Nashua, NH, Present and Future Facebook page), Amy DeRoche, Billy Fokas, Peter Bouchard, Ron Trudeau, and Chris and Alan Way for sharing their stories and love for Nashua.

I am so grateful for my husband James, our three children-Vincent, Shannon, and Steven, my parents Don and Carol, my in-laws John and Camille, and my extended loving family, who have stood by me every step of the way. This is for my sister Shannon and nephews Owen and Brandon, who share my love for spooky tales, too. I also wish to honor my caring Nashua educators: Stanley A. Stoncius, Walter Heinhold, Linda Richard, Bonnie Phelps, Bob Sherman, Marie Mellin, Deborah Carpenter, Bob DeMello, Silvia Abelleira, Irene Oliveira, Susan Testa, and Stephen Norris from Nashua High School; and Rivier University Professors Patsy Roberts, Susan Gately, and Bradford Stull. Also, much love to my sweet book club friends: Sarah, Kim, Wendy, Lisa, and Brandie for encouraging my passion.

Finally, to my resilient fellow Nashua High School graduates, especially my dear friend Haley, I am grateful for so many memories.

Keep believing. Happy Reading.

Bibliography

Caduto, Michael J, and Joseph Bruchac. *Keepers of the Night.* Fulcrum, 1994.

Fassett, Jame. H. *Early History of Nashua for Fourth Grade.* Telegraph Publishing, Nashua, NH. 1915.

Flythe. Jane, M. *God's Acre: A History of the Old South Burial Ground, Nashua, NH.* Puritan Press, Inc. Hollis, NH. 1988.

Goodale, John H. *The History of Nashua.* 1885.

Hargreaves, Susanna. "Rumors of Hauntings at Nashua's Clocktower Place." Nashua Telegraph, 25 Oct. 2015.

Haven, Robert. *Nashua: A History*, 1 Jan. 1981.

Manoian, Alan. *The History of West Pearl Street and the Tremont House.* YouTube, 19 May 2013, https://youtu.be/Fm690IBxEyA.

Parker, Edward Everett. *History of the City of Nashua, NH.* 1897.

Peters, Ann Robin. *Nashua, Then & Now*. Arcadia Publishing, 2006.

"Rokas Boy Confesses Slaying His Pal." *Nashua Telegraph*, 24 Oct. 1928.

"Astounding Juvenile Murder Revealed By Discovery of Body." *Nashua Telegraph*, 24 Oct. 1928.

"Terrible Conflagration in Nashua! Two Large Factories Burnt!" *Nashua Telegraph*, 1 July 1856.

"Child Injured." *Nashua Telegraph*, 9 Nov. 1880.

"Man Killed in Elevator Fall." *Nashua Telegraph*,13 Jan. 1949.

"Man Shot and Woman Injured." *Nashua Telegraph*,18 Oct. 1915.

"Nashua Police Investigate Second Black Bridge Suicide in 3 Weeks." *Nashua Telegraph*, 21, Feb. 2013.

"Old Burial Ground At Greeley Park." *Nashua Telegraph*,18 May 1907.

"Jim Stivie Beaten Up After Leaving Mills Last Night Dies at Hospital—Cases of Rioters in District Court." *Nashua Telegraph*, 20 Oct. 1915.

"Strikers Reject Proposal of State Labor Commissioner." *Nashua Telegraph*, 15 Nov. 1915.

"Hauntings Remain with Their Houses." *Milford Cabinet Press*, 25 Oct. 2013.

Redish, Laura, and Orrin Lewis. "Abenaki Legends, Myths, and Stories." *Native Languages of the Americas*, www.nativelanguages.org/abenaki legends.htm.

Stack, James, and Jay Hanlon. "Gas Blast Kills Six Nashua Train Hits Truck Loaded with Fuel Tanks." *Union Leader*, 7 Dec. 1960.

Stylianos, John. "Young Nashua Family of Four Is Dead in R.R. Crossing Crash Today." *Nashua Telegraph*, 7 Dec. 1960.

"Uncover Skeleton in School Yard." *Nashua Telegraph*, 12 July 1916.

Susanna Hargreaves is an educator and writer from New Hampshire. Susanna and her husband have raised three children and four dogs on an old, haunted road. And yes, she believes in ghosts. (She once lived on the second floor of the haunted apartment building on West Pearl Street.)

Check out some of the other *Spooky America* titles available now!

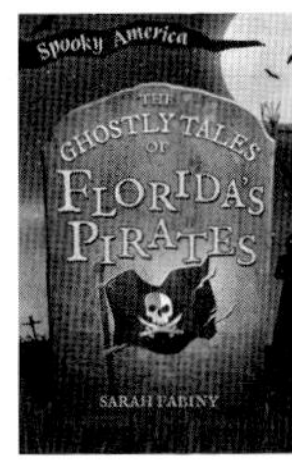

Also by Susanna Hargreaves: